If you can be anything, be kind

Poetry and photographs
by Stephen Quinn

Typeset in Century Schoolbook

All photographs by Stephen Quinn (except the one on page 8 by Sharron Lovell)

Cover photographs by Stephen Quinn

Text copyright Stephen Quinn 2018, who asserts his moral rights as author

Published by MOJO Media Insights, Brighton

If you can be anything, be kind

Stephen Quinn

Acknowledgements

My thanks go to my friend Mary Allen for her many suggestions about how to improve these poems. She is a constant source of encouragement and embodies the sentiments in the title of this book.

Dedicated to my mother, Betty Quinn, on the occasion of her 90th birthday.

Table of contents

Beijing summer palace	09
Butterfly music	11
Beijing café	13
Mountain gift	15
Silkworm	17
Fado	19
Another	21
A city awakens	23
Inelegant words	25
Acceptance	27
Bliss	29
Intimacy	31
Distance	33
Angel's kiss	35
Stars	37
Swallow knowing	39
First flight	41
Owl alba	43
Pigeons	45
Leaving	47
Normandy swallows	49
A soul remembers	51
Lucky eight	53
Forgiveness	55
Soul song	57

Table of contents continued

Whisky cat	59
Kittens	61
Homecoming	63
Another journey	65
A warrior's gift	67
Oasis	69
Dreamtime	71
Honey music	73
Cornsilk	75
Universe	77
Winter	79
LAX to IND	81
Teddy bear	83
Magic meal	85
Cowrie	87
State of mind	89
Rural life	91
Goodbye	93
For my mother, aged 90	95
About the author	96

A lake in Beijing's Summer Palace, by Sharron Lovell

Beijing Summer Palace

Lotus plants are dying in a green lake: Leaves
curling into giant cups, their crinkled edges
laughter lines around the eyes of old men.

Trees like emperors kept erect by iron stairs.
Branches bind across paths, providing ease
for squirrels. Grandfathers with jet black hair

bribe future leaders with ice cream. Leaves spiral
into watery embrace. Carp flash gold, soft song
of life. Bamboo and herons glow in the paintings

of Master Zhang Daqian: His lotus are full of life,
his lakes clear, his trees and mountains strong.
Such knowledge and skill take time to acquire.

Smiles in the central market, Yangon in Burma

Butterfly music

Near Po Lin monastery I walk alone.
Mist and cloud cover the Wisdom Path.

It came quickly, like a greedy lover. My
jaw forced wide; a soft breath inside.

Absolute   silence.

Then, like
a radio resuming after a power cut:
Birdsong and soft hum of cicadas.
The sweet smell of damp earth,
and the skin-feel of a cool breeze.

I can hear the music of butterflies.

Street scene, Beijing. Nappies are rare in China.

Beijing café

The waitress picks her nose, awaiting my order.
The café walls shake in tune with the traffic.
Students chant, cheerlessly rehearsing lessons.
Slim-hipped *xiao san* snake between tables.

Outside, an old man gentles a Mongoloid child
through traffic. The sky blossoms grey-brown.
A woman watches her grandson shit in the street.
Nappies are rare, toddlers with slits in their pants.

Where is the birdsong? The sparrows have been eaten.
Where are the ancient buildings? Adorned with smog.
Where is the wisdom of the Tao? Fighting to be heard.

When it rains I taste the bitterness of progress. Rivers
and gutters carry away many kinds of dreams.

* *xiao san* is Mandarin for mistress, as in "little three" or third person

* In China many deformed children are aborted or kept at home if born; it is rare to see a less-abled child in public

A faded Mao uniform near Yunnan province, China

Mountain gift

The chocolate we shared on Moon Mountain was sweet,
my sadness an echo from previous lives. Are creeks
carved into mountains just tears? Laughter followed:
Sunshine after rain. We spoke of mountain spirits.
Calmed by the sweet green of your voice and eyes,
I heard the mountains and rivers sing.

As a child my world and heart were small.
As a man they expand with time. The beauty
of Yangshou's rivers and mountains touched
my soul, gave me peace. Why need feel sad?
I have love to give. And a world to give it to.
Such a gift only really needs one receiver.

A woman in Yunnan province, southern China

Silkworm

It was easy being asleep.
A chrysalis-curled soul
ignoring the world.

Now the kiss of hope
awakens the deepest
of silken slumbers.

Your echoes haunt me:
Hints of a dark continent
we came to know as love.

I suspect I fear you. The
you who has disturbed
my uneasy equilibrium.

Lunch sometimes requires a bit of culinary gymnastics

Fado

He plays fado in Macau's museum of wine.
Eyes smiling, head turned lightly to the sky.

Clink of Cantonese. Mahjong tiles and smoke.
He winks at me and smiles: "Finally we flow!"

In another life my son sings a guitar and I weep,
missing the music of a child's love and being.

* Fado (Portuguese for "destiny" or "fate") is a music genre associated with longing for home. The Portuguese *guitarra*, a plucked instrument with 12 steel strings, is usually used to play fado.

A face of kindness in Fujian, Suzhou province

Another

Blue skies over sunny Suzhou,
sweet city of silk and canals.
It's the place I came to know
how kindness can help us grow.

At the back of the bus I sat alone
A Westerner with a serious frown.
An old man gave me an apple, ripe
like his face, a gentle act of grace.

Life outside was chaotic: Traffic like
a man gone berserk. Yet that act
froze time, transforming my view
of how we need to be on this Earth.

Friends near Lijiang city, Yunnan province, China

A city awakens

The world divides: people prepare for bed or greet the day.
At 5am this city's streets are busy. Old women wake,
drink their scented tea, ready to play with grandchildren.

Nose nuzzling carpet a Muslim prostrates towards Mecca.
A man in tight jeans and white Crocs ushers a woman
to his apartment door, hoping for more than coffee.

An old man trundles a trolley filled with toys for his stall.
The 7-11 staff yawn and stretch as they stack the shelves.
A city's awakening is a mix of miracles and the mundane.

A Buddhist monk outside his monastery in Macau

Inelegant words

Our journey to love began slowly:
To know your independent quirky
ways took me some time to acquire.
My rumpled casual emotional style
required much tolerance to admire.

My rhyme is tortured, my scansion poor
desperate to connect, my words ignore
the need for elegance – your trademark.
It's one of many things about you I adore
as I welcome the chance to open my heart.

A carpenter in Lijiang's central market, Yunnan

Acceptance

Alone I walked in a garden of roses
one summer's night decades ago.
Colours trilled and aromas glowed.
It should have been a time of awe.

Yet in this place of beauty I saw
only decay. Each bud had flaws.
No rose would ever be enough
for a man so fully incomplete.

That garden beheld a creature
unable to accept himself. But
over the years your gift of love
helped me see I am replete.

Lotus harvest, Humble Administrator's Garden, Suzhou

Bliss

Perfect orchids, pink against azure sky,
sit serenely in the sunlight of my mind.

My body murmurs in awe with the find:
Secular beauty embracing the divine.

To convey the bliss the petals provide
is futile, like containing mercury's slide.

Words dissolve like tissues in the rain.
Only the glory of those orchids remains.

The vast lake in Hangzhou, capital of Zhejiang province

Intimacy

What's this thing called intimacy?
It's not clear, yet I know its colour:
The soothing blue-grey madrigal
of your eyes on a summer's night.

I know its feel: It's the brush
of your lips against my neck.
Or the swaying of our bodies
in the dark beauty of the night.

I know its texture and taste:
Sweeter than any Sauternes,
richer than any vintage port.
A ravished flood of flavours.

I know its sound: the chuckle
in your voice and your laugh,
when against the flow I know
all that I am meant to know.

Woman in village near Ningbo, Zhejiang province

Distance

We are so close, and yet so far apart.
Miles and oceans separate yet bind.
The distance creates a deeper kind
of longing: An opening of the heart.

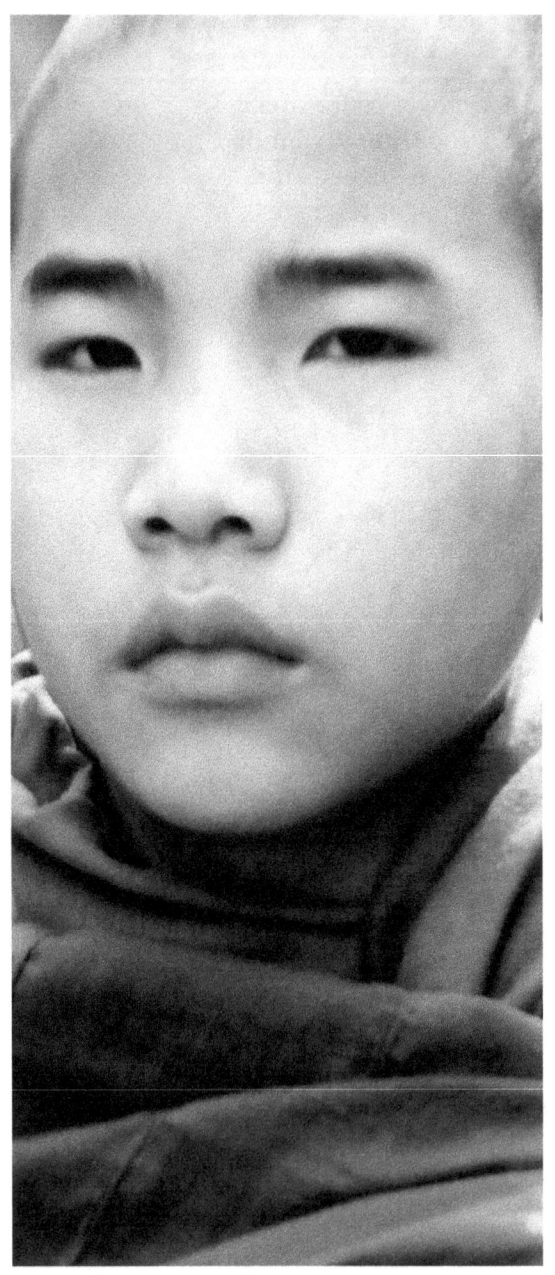

This monk in Myanmar seems so young

Angel's kiss

An angel whispered to me as in a dream:
From love we came and to love we aspire.
We're holograms of light, already supreme.

Her words filled my heart with sacred fire:
Like flowers we grow with and through love,
we're created for joys we know little of.

I cherish the grace those whispers provided:
It's time to accept you're a fragment of god.
Time to awaken, to know the heaven inside.

Dai men discussing life in Yunnan, southern China

Stars

What do they see, these eyes of the sky?
What do they hear? The humming of tyres
on a distant road. Scratch of pen on paper.
The croak of lonely frogs in a distant acre.

What do those eyes feel? Tenderness
or pity? Awe? Or maybe just contempt?
Probably a delicate indifference.
The stars are always somewhere else.

Demolition near Ningbo, China

Swallow knowing

A small child runs into the setting sun.
Chase me daddy. See how fast I can run.

Silhouettes of swallows over the meadow.
Memories of time, an etching on an urn.

My daughter stumbles, rolls ... recovers
and runs into the golden light. I love her

unknowing, and wonder what she'll learn
with time. Is it also so for the swallows?

Sharing photos on the Bund in Shanghai, China

First flight

A baby bird at edge of nest:
Does it need to think before
taking its maiden flight?

Human eyes lock in love
across that crowded room:
Need they fear the future?

Blind poets conjure stories:
Is it because they see things
they should not speak of?

Like foggy mirrors after a bath
fear shrouds a sense of self. We
shape a future in steamy glass.

Choice is all we have: To believe
in possibility and leap without
fear into unknown possibilities.

Thought I took this photo without their noticing

Owl alba

A wide slice of melon moon, white in starry dawning,
shadows the field where the owl hunts this morning.

The village is monochrome at the start of the day.
Buildings of white stone reflect the moon's play.

The light whispers and the sky echoes white gold.
The owl's answer is like a man mourning his soul.

Talons release. The owl drops from a branch, aching
in an arc of silver light, now silent yet fully knowing.

In a dream I'm driving in Jordan's capital, Amman.
The feast of Eid al-Fitr marking the end of Ramadan.

Sheep slaughtered in streets, meat given to the poor.
My car slides in blood, red wetness splatters the door.

We humans fashion nests from wood, stone and clay.
Owls need no stones; they create their own way.

Life's about choice, like words ordered in a poem.
A poet ponders on life while the owl hunts alone.

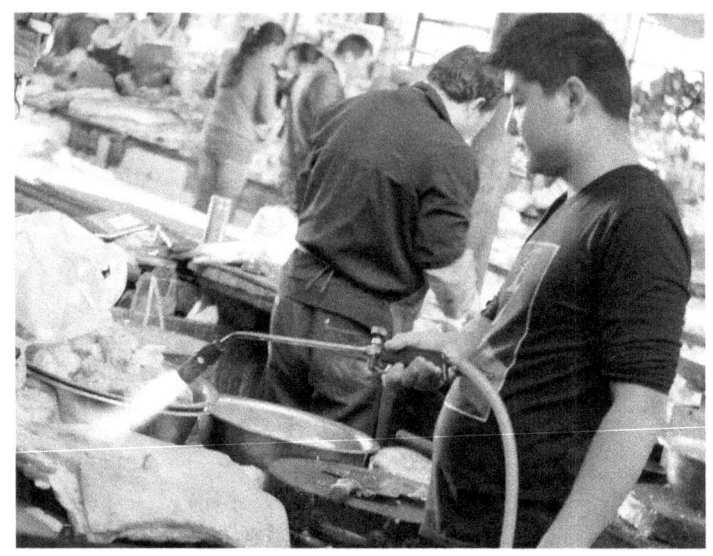

A blowtorch to remove pork bristles at a market

Pigeons

I watch pigeons from a window of my Hong Kong flat.
Communal creatures, they coo like Filipino maids
at Central on Sundays, gathering for a fashion parade.

Among the maids I spy only women. Feathery frisson
announces the arrival of a male. Chest pushed proud,
he pursues a target, an eight snaking into the crowd.

The first ignores this dance of desire and flies off.
He preens and selects another. Is he driven by lust?
From a distance he seems rather ridiculous.

The second hen accepts and their coupling tumbles
through time. Is it desire, or nature's necessity?
I ponder alone and palely loitering, a voyeur of birds.

Bus stop at a remote village, Zhejiang province

Leaving

Bats always turn left when leaving a cave.
Survival guides their flight. Humans escape
in subtler ways, even when they say they'll stay.

For you, leaving revealed your need for survival:
Executed like sonar, precise in flight, unexpected.
The desire for freedom your greatest work of art,

for love flies straight and hard when it departs.
The strongest muscle in a body may be the tongue,
but surely the toughest must be the human heart.

The morning after, Hanoi, Vietnam

Normandy swallows

My favourite word when learning French
at high school those many decades ago
was *l'hirondelle*, the swallow. A word sent
to conjure joy with its magical flow.

Swallows skim above our Normandy gite
the arc of their flight immeasurably sweet.
As we sip our wine the swallows glow bright.
Both link us with heaven, angels in flight.

Securing the load, a common sight in central China

A soul remembers

A soul remembers its source when met with love.
Passion is not suffering, but the conquest of fear.
Fear not for I am with you. I am with you always.

A baby bird on edge of nest already knows
how it is made for flight. Forget fear and fly.
Tremble not, for your soul will remember.

Like flight for the bird we have little to learn.
We yearn for self-knowing, that mighty leap
into eternity. Ready for a life we already know

without knowing. We are love first and last, alpha
and omega. We have lived many times, yet each
life remains new-found, like waking at dawn.

A man waits for his dinner, Shangri-La, China

Lucky eight

Like nutmeg in a dream, the memory of you
lingers longer than any expensive perfume.

Naked and alone I sleep, yet the flow of you
warms my soul like the taste of honey dew.

I held your luscious body and remember it still:
A chicane of tight curves and sensuous trills.

Soon I will sleep, a man complete and content
scratching eight lucky lines to mark the event.

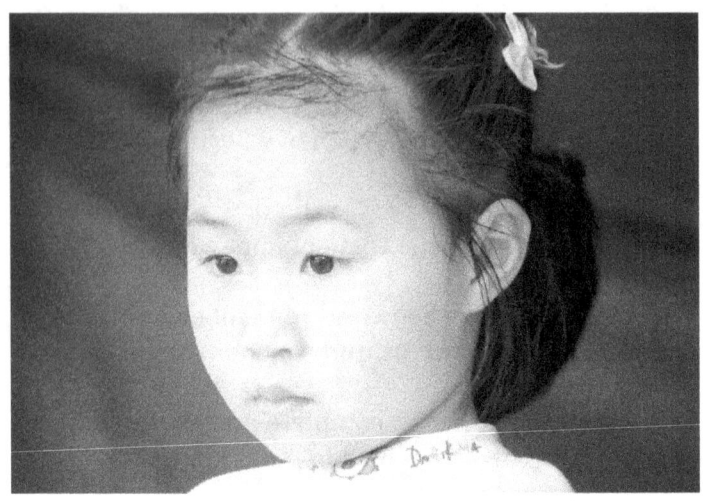

A child in Yangshou, near Guilin, Guangxi province

Forgiveness

My lover rejects me for a crime
from another life, a darker time.

Ancient ways of hate can dictate
the chance for freedom in this life.

Can we free ourselves and others
from forgotten sins yet uncovered?

A memory of another's fiercer pain
helps us accept the need to forgive.

Tourists rafting on the Li River in Guangxi province

Soul song

Candles gutter. Dynasties fade. Tears dry. Surely we know the dawn will come. Life continues and seasons unfold. Hope remains, more joyous than any birdsong, more profound than any book, sweeter than any love affair.

Early morning tai chi meditation, Shanghai

Whisky cat

Whisky slips down my throat:
Purring promise of peaty regret.
The brown cat of oblivion
sleeps curled by the fire.
Memory beckons me to forget.
I am alone, and all is fine.

Guilin's River Li is a popular place for weddings

Kittens

Kittens are tangling the wires of my television,
buggering my reception, shrouding perception.

Laurel is lean and Hardy is fluffy. They rocket
after each other, exploding bristle brushes.

They chase moths and other creatures of the night
and afterwards trill softly, beckoning to the light.

They sail like silk from couch to rug, ungainly
Leaping like suicides yet always landing safely.

Do these kittens know how serious their play?
They live for now, for they only have today.

How I envy them their innocent now-ness.
Those kittens who jangle my perception.

Women enjoying the sun in Shangri-La, southern China

Homecoming

Snails of snot on the moonlit window
tells me the cats have been waiting.

The neighborhood slumbers. A siren
pleads: A prostitute desperate for cash.

Discarded pizza boxes prepare to sing,
empty DVD cases their backing group.

Cats caress my leg. My stale cigar smoke's
the only perfume in the master bedroom.

The joys of sugar cane in a market, central China

Another journey

The train bolts like a fox freed from captivity.
England's green beauty recedes into eternity.

On the horizon trees caress breasts of clouds.
I find myself humming a love song aloud.

Memories of love and life float about my brain.
Images blurred through the window of a train.

A journey begun years ago offers its refrain:
I know I can love and am able to love again.

In Hanoi, Vietnam: Betel nut or misplaced makeup?

A warrior's gift

I've been a warrior in many lives
and bid farewell to many wives.
I've loved and shed too many tears,
killed and cried for too many years.

Let this old warrior offer you a gift:
Mix wine with joy, and sweetly sing
of life's unfolding bliss. For at close
of day we can only know one thing:

Our lust for love and its linking
overwhelms an already knowing.
Self-love's a more splendid rose
than love from any other being.

A friendly sign in Kunming, capital of Yunnan

Oasis

Tonight I needed you the way a dying man
seeks solace at an oasis of redemption.

We've known each other such a short time.
Yet the flow of your knowing sings deep,

like a wave wide and joyous. It will sustain
through many lives, against many tides.

I cannot hope to seize your love. Like a prize
it is not mine to take, but only yours to give.

A face that has known a full life, near Guilin

Dreamtime

Photos on every wall, ghosts of the past
alive in dreams found forty years after
on the train from Melbourne to Sydney.

Ancient *ficus macrophylla*, Moreton Bay
monsters parasols against time and space.
Fig-ripe summer smells, underfoot squish.

Endless blue skies. Cicada chorus singing
of summer heat. Sighing shrubs flee green
and grey onwards to the horizon. Old trees

like stubble on the faces of ancient hills.
On rocking rails I drift in fitful dreams,
thrown awake by the train's reptilian

squirm. Suburban houses nestle, seeking
warmth. Defrosted dreams leave freezers,
as the Dreamtime rhythm of a wiser me.

Central market in Yangon, Myanmar (Burma)

Honey music

The orchestra buzzes,
a beehive disturbed
by a stick-wielding boy.

The soloist waits, cloth wedged
between chin and violin, its red
matching her silk dress.

The conductor taps a baton.
The swarm surrenders,
fanning embers of the sun.

Fire dances across my eyes.
Blood-hued music, honey
trickling through time.

After three encores
the waves of applause
are beginning to ebb.

He leans from the podium
and kisses the soloist tenderly,
on her sweaty forehead.

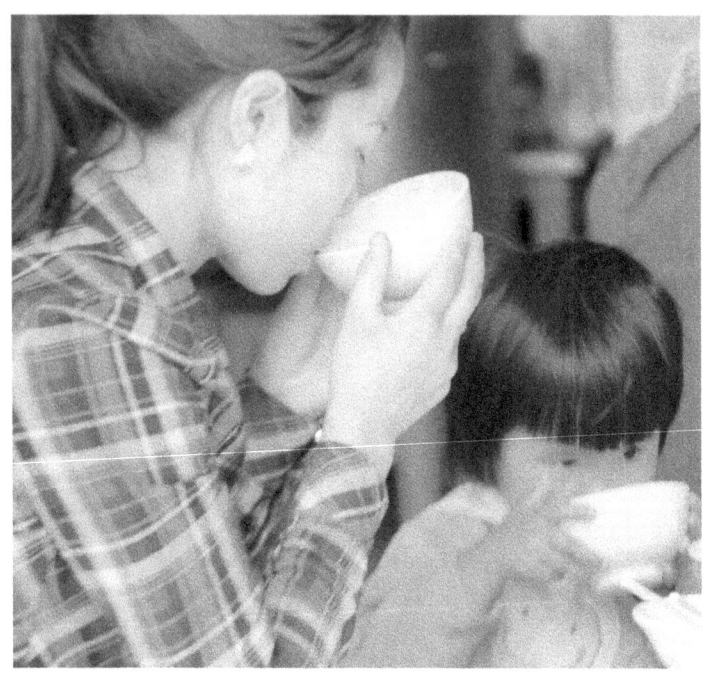

Lunch in Lijiang market, Yunnan province

Cornsilk

Our ferry rode the waves into the city
at close of summer's day.
We sat at the back with wine. It felt
like act one of a play.

Sunlight stroked your shoulders, hair
of warm corn-silk.
Gold strands above the cob proclaimed
how available the fruit.

Fresh flowering of green connection
or tips of vague hope.
With time the strands will darken, yet
another mistaken trope?

Baby navigator in Thimphu, capital of Bhutan

Universe

As I walked home the universe embraced me.
A golden butterfly floated about market stalls.
Joyous in hazard light, it knows how to be free.
A man coaxed an ancient dog on an evening walk.
Confronted with an urge to sing, I rejoice
in the pain of being alive. I'm sublimely glad.
For the universe continues to embrace the mad.

New friends in Fuzhou, Fujian province, China

Winter

Winter sunshine dapples city towers and valleys.
Sunlight's splendour warms my back and face.
An eagle rides the thermals in Hong Kong blueness.
Today I have soared those same skies in ecstasy.
The roar of the traffic fades into insignificance, for
I know the joy of love and its special kind of peace.

Enjoying the sunshine in Thimphu, Bhutan

LAX to IND

Tears condense on window 13A
as I bid farewell to sunshine and love.

The world below a complimentary movie:
California glimmers, a dreamy goddess
of greyness. I admire her breasts and thighs
beneath a patchwork quilt. Violent passions
of mountains and valleys so far away.

She fucks hard under the covers.
Poste coitum triste, I doze and dream
and wake maybe three hours later.
The crooning softness of captain's voice:
"We're approaching Indianapolis,
please fasten your safety belts."

Clouds like roadside sludge
drift by my window, taffy pulled
into a soft Lowry landscape.

The jet becomes a giant's plaything
a second-rate pugilist bobbing and weaving
yet pummelled by a tougher pug.

Landing is a punch to the solar plexus.

Late at night the house is empty and cold,
my only companions a pair of hungry cats
resentful at being ignored. My California
dreaming has become a new reality.

Tiananmen Square, Beijing

Teddy bear

At an early-morning airport
miles and years away from now
a teddy bear smiles at me
from a luggage trolley I follow.

In memory's eye my daughter
clutching another teddy bear
runs to me in morning light
aching to hold her father tight.

Airports are places for leaving
and returning. Yet all too often
they morph into monuments
for remembering and grieving.

Another face that has known life, near Beijing

Magic meal

My daughter offers an empty bowl:
It's really magic soup. Eyes bright
with life she feeds my soul. I sip
the soup with happy heart then

see birthday candles on the floor.
A wad of warm wax is pressed
into my hands. *I prefer sweets.*
She smiles, gaps in her baby teeth.

From soup we move to mains:
A casserole of worms and snails.
Dessert is daisies mixed with dirt,
yellow eyes winking from the mud.

After food, it's time for tunes. Pots
make perfect drums when banged
with wooden spoons. Music creates
another kind of bond. Our black

labrador Harry mountains over us,
tail thumping the tune of the food.
My daughter whoops and smiles again
and I detect a sense of the ineffable.

In Yangshou people seem able to walk on water

Cowrie

My son seeks treasures on my desk.
He cups a cowrie to his ear. Its back,
mottled like his mother's tan, tells
of other summers: Warm coconut oil,

salt lips kissed after sea swimming,
grit of sand in sandwiches. The shell's
curves sang of a season when life
was free, like love and sea breezes.

Disabled musician, Fuzhou, Fujian province

State of mind

At midnight the party brims with people.
Ants scurry across the picnic blanket,
connecting, disconnecting, always hoping.

The master sits among the plastic cups
watching others mingle about the room,
connecting, disconnecting, always hoping.

I stay home alone watching Kung-fu
re-runs. *Remember grasshopper,*
loneliness is only ever a state of mind.

Life is physically hard in Ningbo, Zhejiang province

Rural life

Country of solitude and silence.
Perfumes of trees and stillness.
The feel of green and the clean
sound of wild birds and trees.

Buddhist monks in Yangon, Myanmar (Burma)

Goodbye

An angel asked me: *What is the greatest gift one can give another?* Love, I offered in reply. *Love is already given,* the angel said, *like knowing the sun will rise. Our greatest gift*

is freedom. With it comes choice and hope. Hope sustains us more than food. For we can choose how to live and be. Freedom is saying goodbye when the time is right.

Those words disturbed my heart. *Fear not,* whispered the angel, *life offers many kinds of freedom. Go forth in love, and be free, for that is what your soul yearns to be.*

Let's find champagne to toast a pure soul as we open the doors of awakening hearts. Though at this time we must travel apart, we'll meet again, in another life and role.

Betty Quinn with sons and grandson on her birthday

For my mother, aged 90

She's outlasted all the neighbours, those shadow faces of my childhood. What's your secret, I ask?

She smiles. *Simple really. Something to do, someone to love, something to look forward to.* Her face glows.

A halo of grey hair. A child anticipating Christmas. Despite an ulcered ankle, her eyes brim with hope.

If you can be anything in this world, be kind. She's the kindest person I know, always giving things

away. I used to get angry with her wild generosity, until I saw the anger was my own inability to give.

Stephen Quinn

This is the 30th book Stephen Quinn has published, but it's his first book of poetry. Dr Quinn is professor of mobile journalism at the Westerdals Institute of Film and Media at Kristiania University in Norway. For the rest of the year he is based in Brighton in the United Kingdom, where he runs MOJO Media Insights, a digital consulting company.

Dr Quinn has been a journalist with some of the world's major news organisations in Australia, Thailand, the UK, the United Arab Emirates and New Zealand. He has been a journalism professor in Australia, the UAE, the US and China as well as Norway. He returned to journalism with the South China Morning Post in Hong Kong from 2011 until 2013 before he moved to the UK. There he trains people to make broadcast-quality videos with only an iPhone and makes videos. He has travelled to about 90 countries and writes a weekly wine column.

You can read the wine column and learn more about Stephen Quinn at his web site **http://sraquinn.org/**

www.ingramcontent.com/pod-product-compliance
Lightning Source LLC
Chambersburg PA
CBHW070942080526
44589CB00013B/1610